My Permanent Address in Potemkin Village

Reflections on living and leading with sincerity.

By

Timothy Hagler

© 2016 Timothy Hagler

Contact the author at:
timothy.hagler@yahoo.com

Visit the author's healthcare supply chain and leadership blog at:

http://www.thinkoutsideinsupplychain.com/

Like us on Facebook:

https://www.facebook.com/TimHaglerSupplyChainIQ/

Forward

"I just need it to be that way, Tim... I just need the truth to be the way I need it to be."   Jimmy

I am blessed to have friends that disagree with me. It keeps me sharp and allows me the luxury of a social course correction from time to time as needed. Over time we have grown to be fairly adept at the arguments, or at least we are getting so used to the way we each compose and arrange our thoughts that we know just how to bait the trap. Politics (conservative, liberal, progressive), the big issues (gun control, human rights, taxes, immigration, health policy), religion (Muslim, Christian, Baha'i Faith, Judaism, Atheism), and of course the all-important issue of what barbeque style is superior (North Carolina, South Carolina, Tennessee, Texas, Hawaiian, and Korean) ... All of these topics, regularly presented as the 'Bramah Lock' of our collective intellect, daring each of us to be the ONE who could so artistically pick the tumblers of our opinions that the one consistent truth that each of us knows to exist, would be unlatched, finally to herald the advancing singularity, if not the spiritual translation of the saints itself – hallelujah! And that is how we felt about the intensity of the argument. Until Jimmy got a new house.

Sitting there on Jimmy's great new back porch, looking out over the beautiful back yard that ambled down to his private fishing hole on the river, we toasted his acquisition and then we drank some more... and as such the argument was finally well fueled. In fact, this specific argument, for once in a row, was going my way and to the astonishment of all that were there to witness it, I was able to competently deliver a fact-based, data-driven 'coup de gras' aimed right at the heart of Jimmy's feeble politico defense. Then leaning forward in his chair, he quietly and earnestly said it... "I just need it to be that way, Tim... I just need the truth to be the way I need it to be."

I still considered Jimmy's politics to be way off-base, but I had never heard anything so wrong, capped off with such unassailable sincerity. "I just need the truth to be *the way I need it to be.*"

Yes, it was now obvious that Jimmy's new home had a permanent address in Potemkin Village... I swallowed the rest of my beer in a single gulp and began to process the realization that I might very well be his next-door neighbor.

...

This little book is a collage of reflections and thoughts for anyone who is considering the struggle of leading and living with sincerity. There is a tremendous amount of temptation and pressure to be deceitful, and available reward for the most cunning prevaricators, fabulists, and bull shitters. The path of least resistance is deception, the harder road to travel by far, is to be authentic. After all, George Burns said, "Sincerity - if you can fake that, you've got it made."

Let me help you fake it no more, and you will be a person of integrity that Franklin Delano Roosevelt would be proud of as you will "be sincere, be brief, and be seated."

Please use the space provided in the book to take notes and with a little creative presentation please use these reflections as a way to call a meeting to order and give the attendees a sense of presence.

Dedication

For my wife, Kandy... The most authentic person I know.

Potemkin Village

The original Potemkin Village legend is of disputed historical accuracy but is at least framed by some historical fact.

Grigory Potemkin was a real a Russian military leader and statesman was most certainly a favorite lover of the Russian Empress Catherine the Great. According to the legend, however; Potemkin erected fake portable settlements along the banks of the Dnieper River, with soldiers in costume playing the part of productive villagers in order to fool the Empress and her court that the post-war reconstruction of "New Russia" was proceeding well during a journey through Crimea in 1787.

Today, a Potemkin Village is any situation is presented to be better than it really is.

Mind Map

As I brought my thoughts together for this book I used a mind map.

A mind map is a vivid description of a brainstorming session, produced as a diagram of visually organized and connected information. Created around a sentinel concept, drawn as an image in the center of a blank page, to which associated ideas are added. Major ideas are connected directly to the central concept, and other ideas branch out from those.

I am offering my mind map for this book as a help to demonstrate for the reader the vivid connectedness of the concepts presented.

Contents

Forward 3
Dedication 6
Potemkin Village 7
Mind Map 8
Social: "Be" the sincere change 11
Social: (Lie + feeling it)^2 = Truthiness 12
Social: Poe's Law 15
Work: A Bias for Excellence with Action 17
Work: Ship Product 19
Process Improvement: Seeking the thinkers. 21
Colleagues: Care and feeding 24
Colleagues: Post Turtles 26
Calling: A venerable life 28
Work: Self-Reflection 29
Discernment: Deus Ex Machina 30
The Organization: Pushmi or Pullyu 33
Negotiation: To Know Your BANTA – Is to Love Your BANTA 36
Religion: It's good-nuff fuh me 39
Data: Where even the damned liars fear to tread ... 42
Cost Management in Business: If you say so... 45
Life Choices: I am 48
Conclusion 52

Social: *"Be" the sincere change*

"My great panacea for making society at once better and more enjoyable would be to cultivate greater sincerity." — Frances Power Cobbe

If you, like Mahatma Gandhi, felt that "You must be the change you want to see in the world", what would you do first to cultivate the sincere society? The prophet Micah wrote of Balak's consultation with Balaam on how to obtain the favor of Israel's God, that what is required is – "acting with justice, loving kindness, and walking humbly with our God." What a great recipe for sincere living!

Can you think of three personal "requirements" that you can take-up starting this moment, to "be" the sincere change the world needs?

Social: $(Lie + feeling\ it)^2 = Truthiness$

"Repetition does not transform a lie into a truth."
Franklin D. Roosevelt, radio address, October 26, 1939, 32nd president of US (1882 - 1945)

Truthiness was named Word of the Year for 2005 by the American Dialect Society and for 2006 by Merriam-Webster... Truthiness is a quality of an argument or assertion that "sounds or feels right" without regard to evidence, logic, intellectual examination, or facts. Television comedian Stephen Colbert coined the word during an episode of his political satire TV program 'The Colbert Report' on October 17, 2005.

Is that all it takes? Evoke a specific article of insincerity often enough and it becomes socially sincere? Or just make it ring true by making it comfortable through repetition and it will 'become' truth? In a moment, in a twinkling of an eye, this corruption (provided it is repeated often enough) eventually takes on incorruption – because we said so?

In neuroscientific terms, we are talking about cognitive ease, also known as processing or perceptual fluency. The more often a stimulus is repeated, the better primed our brains are to perceive the stimulus fluently, and as such high-frequency stimuli (no matter how true) is translated by our brain into something we can be comfortable with. The ability to harness this effect for our own benefit is also known by its more familiar name as 'intuition.' This is the psychological equivalent of trying to lay down on a single nail that is pointed up. It will obviously hurt you and potentially do some rather uncomfortable damage to delicate skin and tissue. A bed of 10,000 nails, however; will distribute weight with even pressure over the sum of the individual nails and you will not feel discomfort other than your mattress of choice is rather firm. I want to be vividly clear about the difficulties face as we fight natural science when deliberately decoding cognitive ease to try and supplant our intuitive sense of comfort for absolute truth, all for the benefit of NOT automatically falling prey to masterfully placed and repeated stimuli.

Adolph Hitler disagreed with, and openly challenged our opening quote from FDR when he said: "make the lie big, make it simple, and keep saying it and eventually it will be believed."

Fortunately for as much as we are (at times) beholden to the tendencies of perceptual fluency, our best human reasoning, and inherent positivity is "a flame that can be hidden but never extinguished" as Nelson Mandela said.

Unhide your flame today! Let it shine a positive light of truth by off-setting a recurrent lie by repeating a truth!

A real truth – a single nail that sets off a physical and rational reaction to the focused, piercing weight of the emergent issue, not a truth that society at some level decided 'felt enough like the truth' or was amalgamated amongst a bed of repeated, desensitized deceit.

A social exercise in sincerity: Talk with three friends or colleagues, in a face to face group or even an email, text, or instant message group and find one common, sincere, uplifting, truth that should be repeated – and then go to work cascading the message. Even if it is that 'freshly picked, ripe, red, apples taste amazing,' we are getting somewhere.

Social: Poe's Law

Poe's law: *Internet maxim - without a clear indicator of the author's intent, parodies of extreme views will be mistaken for sincerely expressed viewpoints.*

I hate chocolate – LOL.

I hate soft snuggly kittens – NOT!

I love a good hot day with a power outage to keep me from running that pesky air conditioner. ;-)

Do we have the live interaction version of the emoji? Voice inflection? Body language? Eye roll?

Can parody ever be sincere?

To some, 'satire' is the line in the sand that keeps parody honest. Parody is meant to entertain, to poke fun at, while satire is ultimately meant to create a new discussion that will lead to sincere improvement of an actual condition.

Theoretical physicist Richard Feynman said, "The first principle is that you must not fool yourself- and you are the easiest person to fool."

Personally, I am not worried who thinks I am kidding, or who thinks I am serious, and who is mistaking the two... As long as I know that I am not kidding myself!

Work: A Bias for Excellence with Action

"Well done in better than well said."
— Benjamin Franklin

You have developed a reputation for getting things done. You got that reputation by planning your work and working your plan. You certainly believe that there is more value in the 'doing' of the thing, rather than the 'talking about' the thing that needs to be completed. Does that sound like your attitude about your work and accomplishment? Great! You certainly demonstrate a bias for action.

There is a great feeling of workplace acceleration when you get a ton done and really check off the boxes on the 'to-do' list. In fact, that can ensure that you are seen by your company, boss, and colleagues as vital in your position and critical for the success of your team. All good stuff.

Let's explore taking the next step from 'done' to 'well done.' Accomplishing our work with competency is ultimately expected, but a competent accomplishment done respective of high ethics, in cooperative deference to team hand-offs, well communicated, and all done with the positive attitude of an influential leader is deserving of a 'well done.' Work effort well done is the excellence with action that will create your rising tide, lifting all ships and let you shine brighter as a leader that can be considered for progressive responsibilities in the future.

Examine the most recent checked boxes on your do-it list for these qualities of excellent work ethic:

- Respect
- Attitude
- Cooperation
- Appearance
- Character
- Effective Cascading Communication
- Teamwork
- Productivity
- Presence
- Organization

Work: Ship Product

"Blame Nobody. Expect Nothing. Do Something."
- NFL Hall of Famer Bill Parcells

Excellence with action does, indeed, require... you guessed it 'action.' It is imperative to be sincere, respectful, and cooperative, but it is also important to be decisive and courageously ship your product.

How can you get past the over-thinking and over preparing that can breed paralysis, and halt your taking the leap and getting your idea off the drawing board and into a working campaign?

- Fix yourself to the present.
    - Breathe.
- Self-accountability.
    - Be accountable publicly or to others to keep from rationalizing.
- Don't take yourself so seriously
    - When you lighten up you realize that your roadblocks are not so serious either.

- "How…"
  - Not "if."
- Truncate your to-do list.
  - Only the most important things, and keep it short. Brevity begets accomplishment.
- Energize!
  - Emotions can work backward… Communicate and behave like you normally do when you are enthused about your work.
- Do it!
  - Take action, make it happen cap'n!

Process Improvement: Seeking the thinkers.

Matsuo Basho, the great poet of the Edo period in Japan, said "I do not seek to follow in the footsteps of the wise. I seek the things they sought."

"An ant on the move does more than a dozing ox."
– Lao Tzu, seeking small successes that add up more effectively than big campaigns that are held stasis with endless planning or inaction.

"You must be the change you wish to see in the world."
- Mahatma Gandhi seeking sincere expressions of being a living example of change.

"If you can't describe what you are doing as a process, you don't know what you're doing."
- W. Edwards Deming seeking a tactile sense of the present.

"A good hockey player plays where the puck is. A great hockey player plays where the puck is going to be."
- *Wayne Gretzky seeking visionary solutions.*

"If one does not know to which port one is sailing, no wind is favorable."
- *Lucius Annaeus Seneca seeking solid goal setting.*

"Improvement begins with I."
- *Arnold H. Glasow seeking ownership and accountability.*

"If you quit on the process, you are quitting on the result."
- *Idowu Koyenikan seeking vocational connectedness with purpose.*

"When everything is a priority, nothing is a priority."
- *Karen Martin seeking the first thing to put first.*

"A corporation is a living organism; it has to continue to shed its skin. Methods have to change. Focus has to change. Values have to change. The sum total of those changes is transformation."
- Andrew Grove seeking the revolution of evolution.

"The most dangerous kind of waste is the waste we do not recognize."
- Shigeo Shingo seeking to know what we don't know.

What are you seeking today?

Colleagues: Care and feeding

"Everyone has an invisible sign hanging from their neck saying, 'Make me feel important.' Never forget this message when working with people."
– Mary Kay Ash

I worked with an organization that espoused the charism: "know me, care for me, and ease my way." What an eloquent way to describe our best approach to everyone who we engage with… What a sincere way to make sure we are observing the importance of every person.

Good energy tip:

Seek out a quiet colleague and ask them for personal advice or input on a specific project. Example: "John, I have noticed that you always do such a detailed and efficient loading of all the new products into our master file when we implement a new supplier contract… Can you outline some order of supplier information to match your order of operations, and perhaps what additional information we should be gathering? We would be happy to make sure the information we receive from trading partners helps you in your tasks as well."

Good energy tip 2:

Give a colleague an unexpected gift that you know will mean something to them. Example: "Sally, I have heard you comment three times on that motivational poster I keep in my office. I would like you to have it. I know it will be a source of motivation and have deep meaning for you and it would be a pleasure to know it is in such good hands."

Colleagues: Post Turtles

Imagine this... You are driving down a country road, and you come across a fence post with a turtle balanced on top. You stop the car to ponder the situation for a moment. You know the turtle didn't get there by itself, it doesn't belong there, and it certainly isn't going to get anything done while it's up there.

This little visualization is a vivid description of the Peter Principle. The Peter Principle is a concept in management theory formulated by Laurence J. Peter, based on the notion that employees will continue to get promoted as long as they are competent, but at some point they will either fail to get promoted beyond a certain level, because it has become too challenging for them – or worse; they are promoted beyond their level of competency based on past success in lesser roles. At that point, "they have reached their level of incompetence".

When you are ready to take that next promotion, think honestly about your motives by taking a quick sincerity check by reflecting on these three judgments.

Reflective of your new role, are you considered:

A subject matter expert?
A thought leader?
Will this role allow you to demonstrate being a natural and continuous learner?

If so, you are no post turtle! You need to accept that promotion and make great things happen.

Calling: A venerable life

"... live a life worthy of the calling you have received."
- Ephesians 4:1

A job will build a roof over your head. A calling will build a legacy. *What is yours?*

A job will provide food for your table. A calling will provide evidence that you were generous with the human condition. *What does the evidence point to about you?*

A job will make wealth. A calling will make a difference. *If you did not satisfy your calling, who would notice?*

Live so you are recognized by the force that calls upon you.

Work: Self-Reflection

Who we are looking for is who is looking.
- Francis of Assisi

You

Are

Already

Enough

Have faith… The road is rising to meet your steps.

Discernment: Deus Ex Machina

"I find it interesting that the meanest life, the poorest existence, is attributed to God's will, but as human beings become more affluent, as their living standard and style begin to ascend the material scale, God descends the scale of responsibility at commensurate speed."
- Maya Angelou

If we truly believe in divine intervention in challenging times, then shouldn't we also believe that God orders our steps during times when we are doing well?

How many times do we take credit for accomplishment and success, when we have also asked for intervention with the troubles and quirks of life?

Also, the things that are happening to you aren't the definition of "you." They are just the things that you are dealing with… How you deal with them is more defining.

Personally, I believe in divine intervention, but it is hard to profess "God's will" or a "universal rhythm" or any "interventional mechanism" in a sincere manner. The dogma of holy intercession seems to be dotted with the two-faced land mines of hypocrisy. If it is good – "I" did it... if it is bad "the unseen hand" is either punishing me or will guide me through it.

I never felt the blessing of intervention in a profound way, until I opened my heart to honest discernment between surrendering to a self-determinate life, or accepting a life lived with calling and therefore intervention. In acknowledging the latter, I felt immediately grateful for competent participation in all the successes within my life experience, and a sense of being unafraid of the challenges.

My wife also pointed out that "just because something is happening to you, doesn't mean it's about you." Her point was that our trials as well as our victories are also a mirror for others who are struggling, succeeding, and just trying to follow a legitimate calling with devotion, sincerity, and grace. Today, I am in awe of how there is always a way presented to me, to use my experience to help someone else in their walk.

Challenge yourself:

Are you honestly giving way to the sincere application of either some sort of divine intervention? Or are you even honestly resolute in giving credence to an autonomous existence? Either is genuine. But if you are the living example of "deus ex machina" (*where a divine character is introduced into a storyline for the purpose of explaining an improbable resolution to a conflict*), simply explaining away the trials of living as God's will, while taking credit for a "job well done" when things go right – you have some maturation experiences to look forward to. Don't worry, just wait right there, they will be along shortly.

Reflection: What have you experienced that brought you to the realization that you are self-determined, or that you are the ongoing recipient of intervention?

The Organization: Pushmi or Pullyu

"When you're a manager, you work for your company. When you're a leader, your company works for you."
- *Stan Slap*

The pushmi-pullyu is a fun, fictional character from *The Story of Doctor Dolittle*. This strange "gazelle-unicorn cross" has two heads (one of each) at opposite ends of its body. The pushmi-pullyu uses one of its heads to talk, reserving the other for eating, grooming, etc. I think about this critter whenever I talk to a colleague who is in management or has been practicing as a high-level individual contributor, and now they find themselves transitioning into a leader.

Often an emerging leader experiences the disorientation of transition as they move from pushing the organization forward from behind the strategies and tactics published by other management (often long ago), to pulling the organization forward over and around the status quo. That in-between area of 'leadership doldrums', the magnetic field, the area of attraction or repulsion, of an organization between two opposing magnetic poles, is often where an evolving leader first experiences the most radical effects of organizational culture.

As an effective individual contributor you needed a solid "pitch" so your best ideas would blossom into campaigns that created new value for the organization, and as a manager, you built high-reliability work teams of high-contributing individuals who were effective at executing compelling business and operating plans. The budding leader will soon learn that to get out in front of their organization in a meaningful and sustainable way, they need to be able to influence organizational culture.

A sincere leader influences culture by:

- Actions and behaviors.
    - *"The leader does not say, "Get going!" But instead he says, "Let's go!" and leads the way. The leader does not walk behind with a whip; they are out in front with a banner." - Wilfred Peterson*

- What they focus on and to what issues they give attention.
    - *"Tell me to what you pay attention and I will tell you who you are."* - Jose Ortega y Gassettv

- What they reward, and of course what they punish.
    - *"Like any other tool for facilitating the completion of a questionable task, rewards offer a 'how' answer to what is really a 'why' question."* — Alfie Kohn

- How they allocate resources.
    - Mathew 6:21 – *"For where your treasury is, there your heart will be also."*

Negotiation: To Know Your BANTA – Is to Love Your BANTA

"When we argue for our limitations, we get to keep them."
- Evelyn Waugh

I have spent most of my career working in supply chain management for healthcare delivery systems (hospitals, clinics, health systems). I love this work, we are providing for and filling, the hands that heal.

When focusing specifically on optimizing a competitive trading partner environment, I have always gone into discussions being well prepared by knowing my BANTA. Best Alternative to a Negotiated Agreement. This is simply knowing our strongest alternative if potential supplier talks start to get out of my control. Inexperienced negotiators will often try to 'finesse' a negotiation back on track, but that is a fool's game.

Sometimes my BANTA is simply to declare that the talks have taken a drastic off-road turn and we will option for a six-month extension on the current agreement (maybe with a market share kicker on discount so the marketplace resets while you take the time-out) so we can level-set and come back to the table later. Another common BANTA is just to walk away from discussions yourself and move to a pre-bid conference and put the discussions into a public, formal and structured process with a series of toll gates to control the ability of your counterparts to off-road the topics. There are numerous tactics, but all of them are designed to keep one's strongest position available at all times so you never get backed into a corner and have to settle for a weak alternative.

Think about this in any other context of leadership or just 'life in the real world' in general. Actually, many people suffer from a terrible malady that keeps them perpetually in a state of having a "crappy outlook…" It's "butt-eye" disease! (literally "but I")

When you ask why an assignment wasn't completed and the person to whom the task was assigned says - "I would have finished it BUT I need more resources." Or you ask your child why they are ringing wet laying in bed in their pajamas obviously not having dried off after their shower and they tell you - "BUT I didn't hear you tell me to dry off, you just said 'take a shower, get in your PJs and go to bed'..."

When you have 'butt-eye' disease you never even know your best alternatives, you just focus on your limitations and make excuses for them. Is it a wonder why the drama is returned to you? You are simply reaping what you have sown.

Take it from an old 'roll up your sleeves, junkyard dog, battlefield general' of a business negotiator... in any situation, always know your best alternatives and argue only from a position of strength. Because when you argue a weak case you will likely 'win' that case every time.

Religion: It's good-nuff fuh me…

"Until an hour before the Devil fell, God thought him beautiful in Heaven."
— Arthur Miller, The Crucible

I grew up in a family that was heavily involved in American folk music, in fact, I learned to play the five-string banjo at a fairly young age. One evening I was just relaxing on the front porch, picking out a lively version of an evolved spiritual song with roots in black and white Southern spirituals – 'That Old Time Religion"…

*Gimme dat ol' time religion,
dat ol' time religion!
Gimme dat old time religion,
it's good enough for me!*

My dad, who was an ordained minister and a card-carrying 'poop-stirrer' wanted to challenge me (likely to teach me a life-lesson) from that old song. "Is it son?" he asked… "Is what-what dad?" I replied. "Is that ol' time religion 'good-nuff' fuh ya?" (good 'nuff said with some pulpit-worthy emphasis) he continued… "Or did the preacher man just tell ya that's how it is without you thinking about it, and THAT'S 'good-nuff fuh ya? Or did you hear a TV evangelist say soothing and THAT'S good-nuff? Or was it like St Luke wrote, chapter 24, verse 32 when their hearts burned within them while Jeeeesus opened the Scriptures TO THEM? Is Gawd burning something on your heart son, or is that ol' time religion just good-nuf fuh ya?"

Wow, what a sermon! Yet – all I really wanted to do was just wanted to do some front porch pickin' while watching the sun set.

My dad, of course, was right, religion is too personal and too important of a topic to approach it incompetently by just parroting what someone else said about it, based on their personal seeking and their own walk with the Master that they identify with.

I have gathered this thought that has served me as an acid test of sincerity when talking about religion well. Just like Bob Dylan said… "you gotta serve somebody…" All of us serve a Master… Atheists do, Christians do, Jews, Hindu community, Muslims, we all do. So Christians – talk about Jesus, we are not competent to argue about Muhammad, neither are atheists competent to argue that God has no place in our life if it is simply that they have not experienced our lives. So because we all have a perspective, that essentially no one else can possibly share due to the deeply personal and spiritual nature of our walk through this life... Seek what those of old sought (from Basho) and since the topic is too serious for amateurs, be reverent, be cautious, be quiet most of the time, and sow only seeds of love and respect for each other.

Oh... And while I am all but convinced that God likes it when you play the banjo, take a lesson or two anyway. I can tell you from experience that the rest of the family probably has a low tolerance for bad pickin' done loudly.

Data: Where even the damned liars fear to tread

"There are three kinds of lies: lies, damned lies, and statistics."
- Mark Twain's Own Autobiography: The Chapters from the North American Review

A few years ago we all realized that harvesting and managing "Big Data" would be a game changer. The lexicon has certainly fleshed out. We have developed outstanding solutions and a ton of the answers we were **seeking**!

- *Hadoop*
- *Flash Storage*
- *Data Visualization*
- *Data Virtualization*
- *Data Democratization*
- *Tableau*
- *Data Governance*
- *Complex Event Processing*
- *Impala*
- *Whole Earth Model*
- *Data Architecture, Analysis, and Design*
- *Database Management*

- *Business Intelligence*
- *Everything aaS*
- *Data Quality Management*
- *Master Data Management*
- *Data Warehousing*
- *Content Management*
- *Metadata*
- *Contact Data Management*
- *Enterprise Resource Planning (ERP)*
- *Gamification*
- *Hive*
- *In-Memory Data Grid (IMDG)*
- *Internet of Things*
- *Machine Learning*
- *Massively Parallel Processing (MPP)*
- *Online Analytical Processing (OLAP)*
- *Operational Data Store (ODS)*
- *Parallel Data Analysis*
- *Parallel Method Invocation (PMI)*
- *Parallel Processing*
- *Parallel Query*
- *Pig*
- *Storm*
- *Structured Query Language (SQL)*
- *Unstructured Data*

Now; can somebody please help us remember the question?

Cost Management in Business: If you say so…

"Finances are like fireworks: they illuminate the sky even as they go pop." - James Buchan

Consider the "Concorde Fallacy" – also known as the "Fallacy of Sunk Cost." The British and French governments continued to fund the joint development of Concorde aircraft even after it became apparent that there was no longer a compelling economic case to continue developing the project. Building the airplane was a commercial disaster and probably should never have been green-lighted and was almost canceled, but both governments bowed to political pressure to keep the program moving since they had already invested so much resource.

The point is this: economic decisions are made every day, and every day there are lies told about the material benefit or fault of a decision based on faulty logic, such as sunk costs. Mostly because somewhere along the line there is a need to prove that some **past** revenue, cost reduction, or investment cost was and is still of value and accretive to current earnings.

To sincerely discuss and ultimately manage economic issues like financial decision support, and expense reduction, we need to include honest discussion about how fear, emotion and irrational factors (such as luck and happenstance) affect the material outcomes of our financial decisions.

I have heard it suggested that the more sincere expense-level management tool could be the Monte Carlo simulation. In this model, we run potential variables and some estimated contributing or detracting value for each through a broad class of computational algorithms that rely on repeated random sampling to obtain potential numerical results.

Isn't it amazing? Standard expense management initiatives traditionally project against cost, quality, and functional results – yet – for as brilliant as those highly reliable elements seem to be, random variables are necessary to keep us honest.

It comes down to this. It's a dirty trick to blindfold someone with their own money. If you are a leader entrusted with fiscal responsibilities, please present expense management and investment positions sincerely.

Life Choices: I am

"Le mieux est l'ennemi du bien. (The perfect is the enemy of the good.)"
— Voltaire

Talk show host and author, Dennis Prager talks about the "Missing tile Syndrome" as the tendency to focus on what we are lacking versus the overwhelming cache of positive attributes that can propel us into an ever-increasing experience of success and even happiness. The vivid example is when you look at a tile ceiling and notice that one single tile is missing, that missing tile becomes the sole focus and the condition that sets the entire ceiling up as a substandard architectural element. Likewise, an otherwise attractive and highly intelligent person, with a solid future and a great family, who happens to have a pronounced lisp (for example) will walk into a room and hear only articulate, clear-speaking people and they immediately start to feel self-conscious.

My dad was a honest-to-goodness renaissance man, he excelled at many things and he made his living at a number of diverse vocations... Portrait artist, illustrator, photo retoucher, police detective, judge, minister, luthier, radio talk show host, musician, art teacher, poet, author, gunsmith, rancher, farmer, feed store owner... he excelled at all his interests and he had an amazing, diverse life.

I need to level set the story a bit for you to see the full picture of my father. You see, he could use only his mind, his voice, and to a very limited degree his right arm and hand. He was stricken with polio as a child and was a victim of violent auto and horse-back accidents as a young man. He was pretty well "busted up" (using his words) for most of his life. But, to me, he was the most "abled" person I have ever met. Have you ever seen and heard anyone play bluegrass music on a five-string banjo using only one hand? I have, and it was great! *(Dad used to say that he was 'busier than a one-handed banjo player...' I suppose he came from a position of integrity on that!)*

My dad had more missing tiles than any ceiling I have ever seen, yet he never focused on them. He only saw what he was able to accomplish, and kept a detailed mental inventory of all of his available internal resources that could be marshaled to help him accomplish whatever he wanted to.

He was famous for pointing out that in the Bible when Yahweh or Jesus wanted to reveal their deity they would say "I AM." So dad told us that a life journey needs to start with you declaring "I AM." Not "I want to be" or "I will be" but "I AM."

Friends, please…
- Know the depth of your personal asset inventory
- Be the change
- Be the accomplishment
- Be enough
- Be more than enough
- Know that any missing tiles will take care of themselves in time, no need to over-focus or even acknowledge them (my father NEVER acknowledged that he couldn't use either leg or his left arm and hand)

How can you be a sincere self-aware person if you ignore every amazing asset you possess and set the course of your life based only on the limitations imposed by focusing on the solitary or the few missing tiles?

You are... Just as I am!

Conclusion

"What it means to be authentic:
- to be more concerned with truth than opinions
- to be sincere and not pretend
- to be free from hypocrisy: "walk your talk"
- to know who you are and to be that person
- to not fear others seeing your vulnerabilities
- being confident to walk away from situations where you can't be yourself
- being awake to your own feelings
- being free from others' opinions of you
- accepting and loving yourself"
— Sue Fitzmaurice

I decided to take on the struggle of packing my bindle stick and leaving the known entity of my own residence in Potemkin Village, and I was surprised at what waited for me at the end of that exercise in awakening a sincere life.

I learned that who I want to be or what I wish I could experience wasn't important. What is important, is who and what I am. I don't want to get too deep into the whole law of attraction conversation, but the affirmative has started to make a lot of sense to me as I sought out what sincere living is all about. I discovered that to think about how much I want to be happy someday, only rewards me with more feelings of wanting to be happy. But when I am grateful for the things and people in my life that surround me with love, and I think about how I am receiving happiness, that is the result... I receive happiness. It is neither authentic or sincere to 'want' something to happen... The only authentic approach is to be the change, to be free from hypocrisy and walk your walk because... 'you are.'

I became more spiritual but less religious. I am more positive and affirming, and less cynical. I am happier, calmer, more trusting, and very grateful... But most of all... 'I am.'

I wish for you to find out that 'you are' too.

Blessings

Tim

Timothy Hagler is an experienced life sciences supply chain leader, with an ever-accelerating interest in earnestly connecting stakeholders with creative ideas to meet new economic realities for healthcare providers. Tim has enjoyed an excellent track record of achievement and advancement earned through demonstrated contribution to bottom-line results, employing strong solutions architecture, analytic and financial skills in a challenging, multi-client environments.

Tim and his lovely wife Kandy enjoy spending time at the beach in South Carolina. Tim's hobbies include photography, illustration (for example all of the line-art style illustrations for this book), American folk music, and writing about himself in the third person.

www.ingramcontent.com/pod-product-compliance
Lightning Source LLC
Chambersburg PA
CBHW070408190526
45169CB00003B/1165